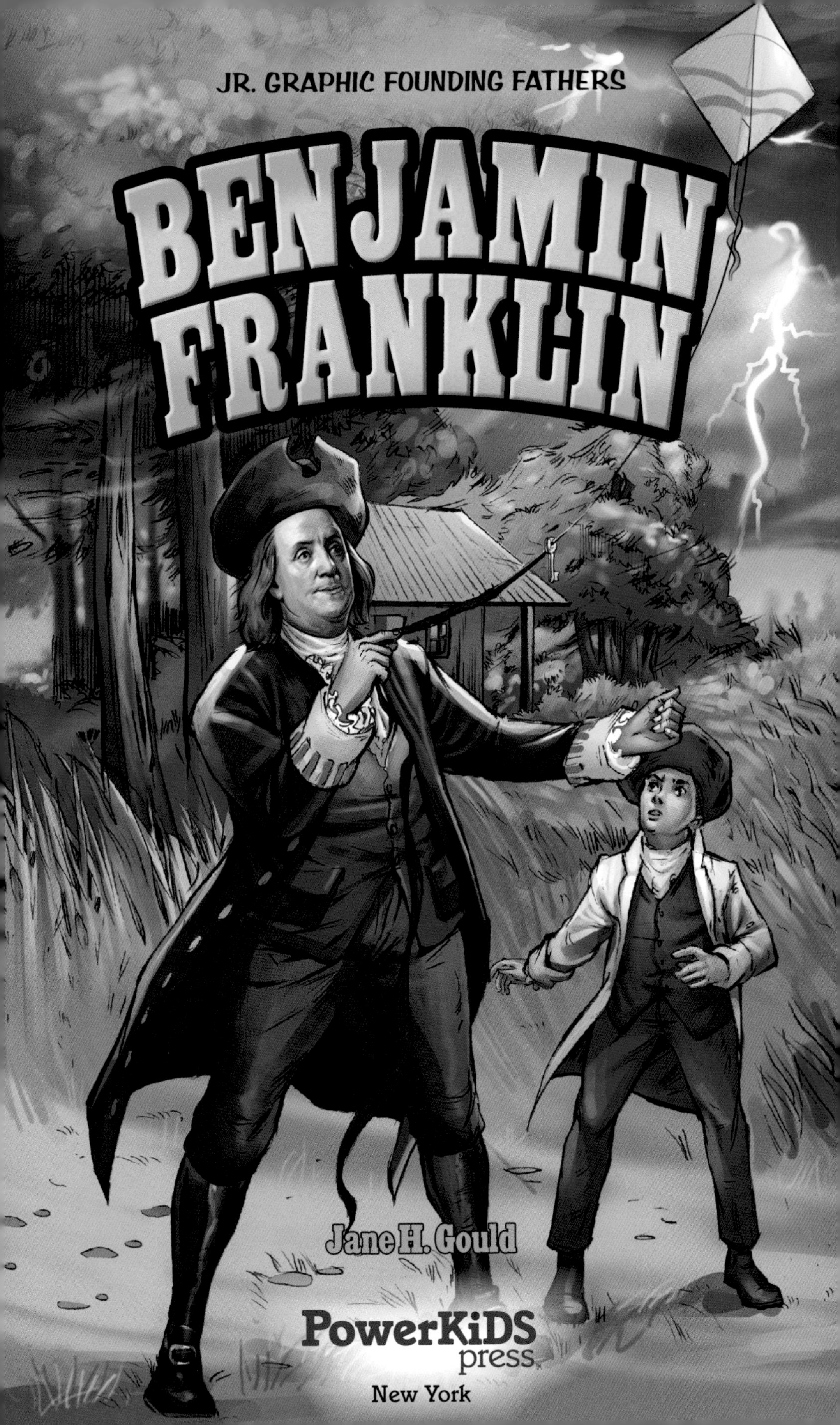

JR. GRAPHIC FOUNDING FATHERS

BENJAMIN FRANKLIN

Jane H. Gould

PowerKiDS press
New York

Published in 2013 by The Rosen Publishing Group, Inc.
29 East 21st Street, New York, NY 10010

First Edition

Editor: Joanne Randolph

Book Design: Planman Technologies

Illustrations: Planman Technologies

Library of Congress Cataloging-in-Publication Data

Gould, Jane H.

Benjamin Franklin / by Jane H. Gould. — 1st ed.

p. cm. — (Jr. graphic Founding Fathers)

Includes index.

ISBN 978-1-4488-7896-3 (library binding) — ISBN 978-1-4488-7990-8 (pbk.)
— ISBN 978-1-4488-7996-0 (6-pack)

1. Franklin, Benjamin, 1706-1790—Juvenile literature. 2. Statesmen—United States—Biography—Juvenile literature. 3. Inventors—United States—Biography—Juvenile literature. 4. Scientists—United States—Biography—Juvenile literature. 5. Printers—United States—Biography—Juvenile literature.
I. Title.

E302.6.F8G6778 2013

973.3092—dc23

[B]

2011048438

Manufactured in the United States of America

CPSIA Compliance Information: Batch # SW12PK: For Further Information contact Rosen Publishing, New York, New York at 1-800-237-9932

Contents

Introduction

Benjamin Franklin was the oldest of the Founding Fathers. By the time the United States declared independence, he was 70 years old. Over his long career, he went from printer's **apprentice** to businessman to scientist and **statesman**. Though he had little schooling, he always tried to study and improve himself. He also wanted to improve the lives of his fellow citizens. His ideas helped the United States become a country that was respected by the rest of the world.

Main Characters

Benjamin Franklin (1706–1790) An inventor, statesman, and diplomat. He helped write the Declaration of Independence and worked to ensure the passage of the US Constitution.

Deborah Read Franklin (1708–1774) Wife of Benjamin Franklin.

Josiah Franklin (1657–1744) Benjamin Franklin's father. He came to the colonies from England in 1682.

William Franklin (1730–1813) Benjamin Franklin's son. He served as the royal governor of New Jersey. He did not share his father's views on independence, remained a Loyalist, and in 1782, moved to London, England. He never returned to the United States.

BENJAMIN FRANKLIN

BENJAMIN FRANKLIN WAS BORN ON JANUARY 17, 1706, IN BOSTON, MASSACHUSETTS. HE WAS THE YOUNGEST SON IN A VERY LARGE FAMILY.

BEN'S FATHER, JOSIAH, MADE CANDLES AND SOAP. HE WANTED BEN TO GO TO SCHOOL TO BECOME A MINISTER. HE KNEW BEN WAS VERY SMART.

MAY I FINISH THIS PAGE BEFORE BED, FATHER?

YES, BEN. IT'S ALWAYS GOOD TO IMPROVE YOURSELF.

BEN ALSO LOVED TO SWIM AND FISH. HE EVEN INVENTED SWIMMING PADDLES FOR HIS HANDS SO HE COULD SWIM FASTER.

I COULD BEAT YOU IN A RACE WITH THESE!

SOMETIMES BEN GOT INTO TROUBLE. HE AND HIS FRIENDS STOLE LARGE STONES TO BUILD A DOCK NEAR A POND WHERE THEY FISHED. THEY HAD TO GIVE THE STONES BACK.

FATHER, THE DOCK IS USEFUL FOR STAYING OUT OF THE MUD.

NOTHING IS USEFUL THAT IS NOT HONEST.

JOSIAH WAS A GOOD FATHER, BUT HE COULD NOT AFFORD TO SEND BEN TO SCHOOL FOR VERY LONG. WHEN BEN WAS 10, HE STARTED TO WORK AS HIS FATHER'S ASSISTANT.

I'M ALMOST FINISHED FILLING THE CANDLE **MOLDS**, FATHER.

THANK YOU, BEN. I NEED YOU TO DELIVER SOME PACKAGES NEXT.

BEN WAS NOT HAPPY WORKING IN HIS FATHER'S CANDLE SHOP. HE WANTED TO BECOME A SAILOR. JOSIAH LOOKED FOR A BETTER **TRADE** FOR HIM.

WHY CAN'T I GO TO SEA LIKE MY OLDER BROTHER?

IT IS A HARD AND RISKY LIFE.

BEN AND HIS FATHER LOOKED AT MANY TRADES FOR HIM, BUT BEN WAS NOT HAPPY WITH ANY OF THEM. HE TRIED WORKING FOR HIS UNCLE, WHO WAS A KNIFE MAKER.

BEN SHOWS NO INTEREST IN MAKING KNIVES.

I WISH I COULD AFFORD TO SEND HIM TO SCHOOL.

SINCE BEN LIKED TO READ, HIS FATHER HAD AN IDEA.

YOUR BROTHER JAMES BROUGHT THIS PRINTING PRESS FROM ENGLAND. YOU COULD HELP HIM PRINT BOOKS.

WHEN BEN WAS 12 YEARS OLD, HE BECAME HIS BROTHER'S APPRENTICE. HE FOUND THAT HE LIKED PRINTING.

YOU MUST PROMISE YOU WILL WORK UNTIL YOU'RE 21.

YOU WILL LIVE WITH ME. IN RETURN FOR YOUR WORK, I WILL GIVE YOU MEALS AND CLOTHES.

AT FIRST, BEN CLEANED THE SHOP AND RAN ERRANDS. SOON HIS BROTHER TAUGHT HIM MORE ABOUT PRINTING.

BEN HAD TO WORK LONG HOURS AS A PRINTER, BUT HE STILL WANTED TO STUDY. HE READ NEWSPAPERS THAT HIS BROTHER PRINTED. HE BOUGHT AND BORROWED BOOKS.

IN 1721, BEN'S BROTHER STARTED HIS OWN NEWSPAPER. BEN WANTED TO WRITE ARTICLES FOR IT. HE TAUGHT HIMSELF HOW TO WRITE BETTER.

BEN KNEW HIS BROTHER WOULD NOT LET HIM WRITE FOR THE NEWSPAPER. HE BEGAN SECRETLY WRITING ARTICLES AND SIGNING THEM "SILENCE DOGOOD." HE SLID THEM UNDER THE SHOP DOOR.

AH, LOOK, HERE'S ANOTHER ARTICLE BY THAT WOMAN SILENCE DOGOOD.

JAMES PUT THE ARTICLES IN THE NEWSPAPER. THEY WERE VERY POPULAR WITH HIS READERS. NO ONE IMAGINED THAT A 16-YEAR-OLD BOY HAD WRITTEN THEM.

HAVE YOU FOUND OUT WHO THIS WOMAN IS?

I WISH I KNEW. THE ARTICLES ARE SO CLEVER!

JAMES'S NEWSPAPER OFTEN MADE BOSTON'S OFFICIALS ANGRY. SOMETIMES THEY PUT HIM IN JAIL BECAUSE OF HIS ARTICLES. WHEN THAT HAPPENED, BEN RAN THE SHOP BY HIMSELF.

HOW LONG HAS JAMES BEEN GONE?

A MONTH. I CAN GET THE NEWSPAPER OUT ALL BY MYSELF.

BEN FINALLY TOLD HIS BROTHER THAT HE WAS SILENCE DOGOOD. JAMES WAS ANGRY WITH BEN. THEY BEGAN TO FIGHT A LOT. BEN DECIDED TO BREAK HIS CONTRACT AND RUN AWAY.

IN 1723, FRANKLIN LEFT BOSTON. HE TRAVELED OVER 300 MILES (483 KM) TO PHILADELPHIA. WHEN HE GOT THERE, HE WAS FILTHY, TIRED, AND HUNGRY.

FRANKLIN SOON FOUND A JOB AS A PRINTER. HE ALSO FELL IN LOVE WITH A YOUNG WOMAN NAMED DEBORAH READ. SHE WAS HIS LANDLADY'S DAUGHTER.

FRANKLIN AND READ WANTED TO MARRY, BUT FRANKLIN DECIDED TO START HIS OWN PRINTING SHOP FIRST. IN 1724, HE GOT HIS CHANCE. THE GOVERNOR OF PENNSYLVANIA LIKED HIS WORK.

I WILL HELP YOU SET UP YOUR OWN SHOP. I NEED A GOOD PRINTER.

I PROMISE THAT YOU COULD FIND NO ONE BETTER.

GOVERNOR KEITH TOLD FRANKLIN THAT HE SHOULD GO TO LONDON TO BUY PRINTING SUPPLIES. HE PROMISED TO HELP FRANKLIN GET MONEY FROM ENGLISH INVESTORS. WHEN FRANKLIN ARRIVED IN LONDON, THOUGH, HE FOUND THAT KEITH HAD LIED. THERE WAS NO MONEY.

I DON'T HAVE ENOUGH MONEY TO GO HOME OR TO STAY IN LONDON.

I'M SURE YOU CAN FIND WORK WITH A PRINTER HERE.

BENJAMIN FRANKLIN FOUND WORK AND ENJOYED LIVING IN LONDON. IT TOOK HIM ALMOST TWO YEARS TO EARN ENOUGH TO SAIL BACK TO PHILADELPHIA. HE FOUND THAT DEBORAH READ HAD MARRIED SOMEONE ELSE.

YOU WROTE ONLY ONE LETTER. I THOUGHT YOU HAD FORGOTTEN ME.

I HAVE BEEN A FOOL, DEBORAH. CAN YOU FORGIVE ME?

IT WAS NOT LONG BEFORE BENJAMIN FRANKLIN WAS ABLE TO START HIS OWN PRINTING SHOP. BY 1729, HE ALSO STARTED PRINTING AND WRITING HIS OWN NEWSPAPER, THE *PENNSYLVANIA GAZETTE*.

IN 1730, FRANKLIN BECAME THE OFFICIAL PRINTER FOR PENNSYLVANIA'S GOVERNMENT. ONE OF HIS JOBS WAS PRINTING PAPER MONEY. HE WAS SO GOOD AT IT THAT NEW JERSEY HIRED HIM TO DO THAT, TOO.

DEBORAH READ'S HUSBAND LEFT HER. SHE AND FRANKLIN FINALLY MARRIED.

I BELIEVE MY HUSBAND WILL NOT BE COMING BACK.

THEN I BELIEVE WE SHOULD GET MARRIED. IT WAS MEANT TO BE.

IN 1732, FRANKLIN **PUBLISHED** ONE OF HIS MOST FAMOUS WORKS, *POOR RICHARD'S ALMANACK.*

Poor Richard's
ALMANACK
1732

ALMANACS WERE PRINTED YEARLY. THEY HAD CALENDARS AND INFORMATION LIKE WEATHER PREDICTIONS IN THEM. FRANKLIN'S OFFERED HUMOR AND GOOD ADVICE.

MY INFORMATION MAY NOT BE ACCURATE. IT WILL, HOWEVER, BE FUNNY!

POOR RICHARD'S ALMANACK HAD THOUSANDS OF READERS. IT WAS SO SUCCESSFUL THAT FRANKLIN PUBLISHED A NEW ONE EVERY YEAR FOR 25 YEARS!

HA, HA! "FISH AND VISITORS SMELL IN THREE DAYS."

I LIKE "EARLY TO BED AND EARLY TO RISE, MAKES A MAN HEALTHY, WEALTHY, AND WISE."

FRANKLIN BECAME MORE SUCCESSFUL AND WELL-KNOWN. HE KEPT TRYING TO IMPROVE HIMSELF. HE ALSO WANTED TO DO SOME GOOD FOR PHILADELPHIA.

I WISH I COULD HAVE BOOKS LIKE YOU GENTLEMEN.

I PLAN TO START A LIBRARY. SOMEDAY, I WANT TO START A HOSPITAL, TOO.

BENJAMIN FRANKLIN CONTINUED HIS **PUBLIC SERVICE**. HE HELPED START THE FIRST ORGANIZED **VOLUNTEER** FIRE COMPANY. MANY MEN JOINED AND IT MADE THE CITY SAFER.

FRANKLIN BECAME POSTMASTER OF PHILADELPHIA IN 1737 AND THEN DEPUTY POSTMASTER OF THE COLONIES IN 1753. LATER, AFTER THE AMERICAN REVOLUTION, HE BECAME THE FIRST POSTMASTER GENERAL OF THE UNITED STATES.

LEARNING WAS IMPORTANT TO FRANKLIN. HE NEVER FINISHED SCHOOL, BUT HE STUDIED ON HIS OWN. HE WANTED PHILADELPHIA TO HAVE A COLLEGE. IT BECAME THE UNIVERSITY OF PENNSYLVANIA.

THIS IS WHERE I HOPE TO START THE NEW SCHOOL, WILL.

AT LAST, OUR BRIGHTEST STUDENTS WON'T HAVE TO LEAVE OUR CITY, FATHER.

FRANKLIN GAVE UP PRINTING TO BE MORE INVOLVED IN SCIENCE AND POLITICS. HE INVENTED A STOVE FOR HEATING ROOMS. NAMED THE FRANKLIN STOVE, IT BECAME VERY POPULAR AND MADE HIM FAMOUS.

THIS IS SO MUCH WARMER THAN A NORMAL FIRE!

IT DOES NOT LOSE HEAT LIKE A FIREPLACE.

THE NEW SCIENCE OF ELECTRICITY CAUGHT FRANKLIN'S ATTENTION. HE PERFORMED MANY EXPERIMENTS. HIS MOST FAMOUS ONE WAS USING A KITE TO GET ELECTRICITY FROM LIGHTNING.

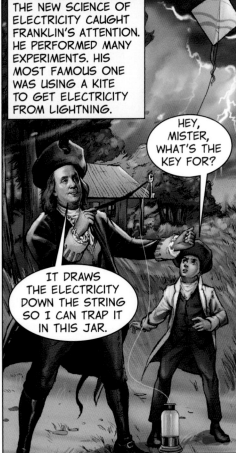

HEY, MISTER, WHAT'S THE KEY FOR?

IT DRAWS THE ELECTRICITY DOWN THE STRING SO I CAN TRAP IT IN THIS JAR.

FRANKLIN WAS **ELECTED** TO SERVE IN THE PENNSYLVANIA **ASSEMBLY** IN 1751. IN 1754, THE FRENCH AND INDIAN WAR BEGAN. THE COLONIES SIDED WITH THE BRITISH AGAINST THE FRENCH.

THE ASSEMBLY SENT FRANKLIN TO ENGLAND. THEY WANTED HIM TO ASK FOR MORE MONEY AND RIGHTS FOR THE COLONY OF PENNSYLVANIA. HE ENDED UP STAYING FIVE YEARS.

FRANKLIN WAS WELL LIKED IN LONDON. HE TRIED TO SHOW THE BRITISH THAT THE COLONIES WERE LOYAL TO THEM, BUT THEY WANTED CERTAIN RIGHTS.

FRANKLIN RETURNED TO PHILADELPHIA IN 1762. TWO YEARS LATER, THOUGH, THE ASSEMBLY SENT HIM BACK TO ENGLAND. FEELINGS BETWEEN THE COLONIES AND THE BRITISH WERE CHANGING.

FRANKLIN ENDED UP STAYING IN ENGLAND FOR 10 YEARS THIS TIME. IN 1765, BRITAIN CREATED A TAX ON THE COLONIES CALLED THE STAMP ACT. FRANKLIN FOUGHT IT AND HAD IT **REPEALED**.

BY 1770, FRANKLIN WAS THE MAIN **NEGOTIATOR** FOR THE COLONIES. HE TRIED TO BE FAIR. AFTER THE BOSTON MASSACRE, THOUGH, HIS OPINION OF BRITAIN GOT WORSE.

RELATIONS GOT WORSE BETWEEN BRITAIN AND THE COLONIES. FRANKLIN RETURNED TO PHILADELPHIA IN 1775. HE WAS IMMEDIATELY ASKED TO JOIN THE **CONTINENTAL CONGRESS.**

DO YOU THINK THERE'S ANY HOPE OF SOLVING OUR PROBLEMS WITH BRITAIN?

NO. I BELIEVE IT IS TIME TO FORM OUR OWN NATION.

FRANKLIN WAS ALMOST 70, BUT HE DID EVERYTHING HE COULD TO HELP IN THE WAR. HE WANTED TO UNITE THE COLONIES IN THEIR FIGHT AGAINST BRITAIN.

WE MUST CREATE A GOVERNMENT THAT CAN RULE ALL THE COLONIES.

I HAVE DESIGNED ONE **CURRENCY** THAT ALL THE COLONIES CAN USE.

OUR ARMY MUST BE ORGANIZED TO FIGHT AS ONE FORCE.

IN 1776, FRANKLIN AND OTHERS HELPED THOMAS JEFFERSON WRITE THE DECLARATION OF INDEPENDENCE. FRANKLIN WAS ALSO ONE OF THE SIGNERS.

YOUR WORDS SHOULD INSPIRE EVERYONE TO SIGN.

SOON AFTER, FRANKLIN WAS SENT TO FRANCE. THE COLONIES NEEDED THE FRENCH TO HELP IN THE FIGHT WITH BRITAIN. IT TOOK TWO YEARS TO CONVINCE THE FRENCH KING TO HELP THE COLONIES.

THE KING HAS AGREED TO GIVE MONEY TO AMERICA.

HE PROMISED **MILITARY** SUPPORT, TOO.

THE AMERICAN REVOLUTION ENDED IN 1781. FRANKLIN STAYED IN FRANCE TO WORK OUT A **TREATY** WITH BRITAIN. THE TREATY OF PARIS WAS SIGNED IN 1783.

BRITAIN NOW RECOGNIZES THE UNITED STATES AS AN INDEPENDENT COUNTRY.

FRANKLIN ENJOYED HIS STAY IN FRANCE. THE FRENCH ADMIRED HIM AS A GREAT SCIENTIST AND PHILOSOPHER. HE WAS INVITED TO ATTEND MANY SOCIAL EVENTS AND WAS WELL LIKED BY EVERYONE.

ONE DAY THESE BALLOONS WILL CARRY MEN.

IMAGINE WHAT YOU COULD SEE FROM THE SKY.

FRANKLIN FINALLY RETURNED HOME, TO PHILADELPHIA, IN 1785. HE WAS 79 YEARS OLD AND IN POOR HEALTH. THE CITY AND ITS PEOPLE GAVE HIM A HERO'S WELCOME.

WELCOME HOME, BEN!

THANK YOU, MR. FRANKLIN!

EVEN THOUGH HE WAS NOT WELL, FRANKLIN ATTENDED THE **CONSTITUTIONAL CONVENTION.** HE WANTED TO HELP SHAPE THE GOVERNMENT OF THE NEW NATION.

DESPITE OUR DIFFERENCES, WE MUST SUPPORT THIS CONSTITUTION.

FRANKLIN FINALLY RETIRED FROM PUBLIC LIFE IN 1789. HE SPENT HIS TIME WRITING AND SEEING FRIENDS. HE ALSO SPOKE OUT STRONGLY AGAINST SLAVERY.

I REGRET THAT I AM TOO ILL TO PRESENT THIS ARTICLE MYSELF.

I WILL MAKE SURE THE **ABOLITIONIST** SOCIETY RECEIVES IT.

BENJAMIN FRANKLIN DIED IN 1790 AT THE AGE OF 84. HE WAS BURIED NEXT TO DEBORAH, WHO HAD DIED IN 1774. MORE THAN 20,000 PEOPLE CAME TO HIS FUNERAL TO HONOR THIS GREAT CITIZEN.

Timeline

1706	Benjamin Franklin is born in Boston.
1718	Franklin starts working as an apprentice for his brother James.
1723	Franklin runs away from his brother's print shop and moves to Philadelphia.
1724–1726	Franklin makes his first trip to London.
1729	Franklin purchases the *Pennsylvania Gazette*.
1730	Franklin marries Deborah Read.
1732	Franklin publishes *Poor Richard's Almanack*.
1751	Franklin is elected to the Pennsylvania Assembly. He also publishes the results of his experiments on electricity.
1754–1763	The French and Indian War is fought.
1757–1762	Franklin goes to England as Pennsylvania's agent.
1764–1775	Franklin returns to England and acts on behalf of the colonies.
1775–1781	The American Revolution is fought.
1776	Jefferson and Franklin help draft the Declaration of Independence.
1783	Franklin signs the Treaty of Paris with Britain, formally ending the American Revolution.
1785	Franklin returns to Philadelphia and attends the Constitutional Convention.
1790	Franklin dies in Philadelphia.

Glossary

abolitionist (a-buh-LIH-shun-ist) Someone who worked to end slavery.

apprentice (uh-PREN-tis) A person who learns a trade by working for someone who is already trained.

assembly (uh-SEM-blee) A group of people who meet to advise a government.

Constitutional Convention (kon-stih-TOO-shuh-nul kun-VEN-shun) A meeting of members from the 13 colonies to create a body of laws for the newly formed United States of America.

Continental Congress (kon-tuh-NEN-tul KON-gres) A group, made up of a few people from every colony, that made decisions for the colonies.

currency (KUR-en-see) Money.

elected (ee-LEK-tid) Picked for an office by voters.

military (MIH-luh-ter-ee) Having to do with the part of the government, such as the army or navy, that keeps its citizens safe.

molds (MOHLDZ) Hollow forms in special shapes.

negotiator (nih-GOH-shee-ayt-er) Someone who tries to reach an agreement between different people.

public service (PUH-blik SER-vis) Work that is done for the good of all people.

published (PUH-blishd) Printed something so people can read it.

repealed (rih-PEELD) Done away with.

riots (RY-uts) Groups of people that are disorderly and out of control.

statesman (STAYTS-man) A person in the government.

trade (TRAYD) The work that a person does.

treaty (TREE-tee) An official agreement, signed and agreed upon by each party.

volunteer (vah-lun-TEER) People who offer to work for no money.

Index

Websites

Due to the changing nature of Internet links, PowerKids Press has developed an online list of websites related to the subject of this book. This site is updated regularly. Please use this link to access the list:

www.powerkidslinks.com/jgff/franklin/